PEOPLE CHANGE Things GO WRONG SHIT happens BUT life GOES ON!

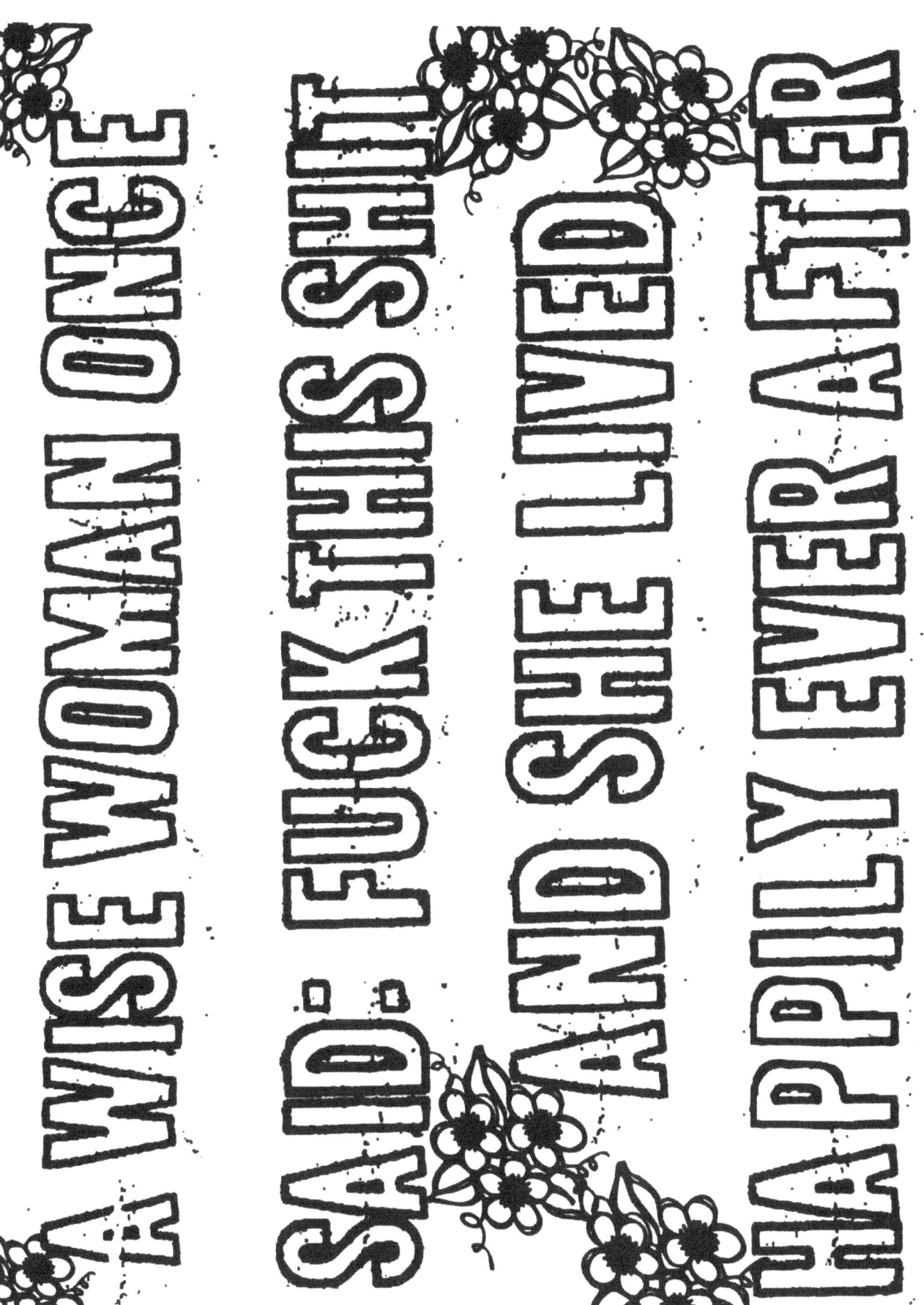

A WISE WOMAN ONCE
SAID: FUCK THIS SHIT
AND SHE LIVED
HAPPILY EVER AFTER

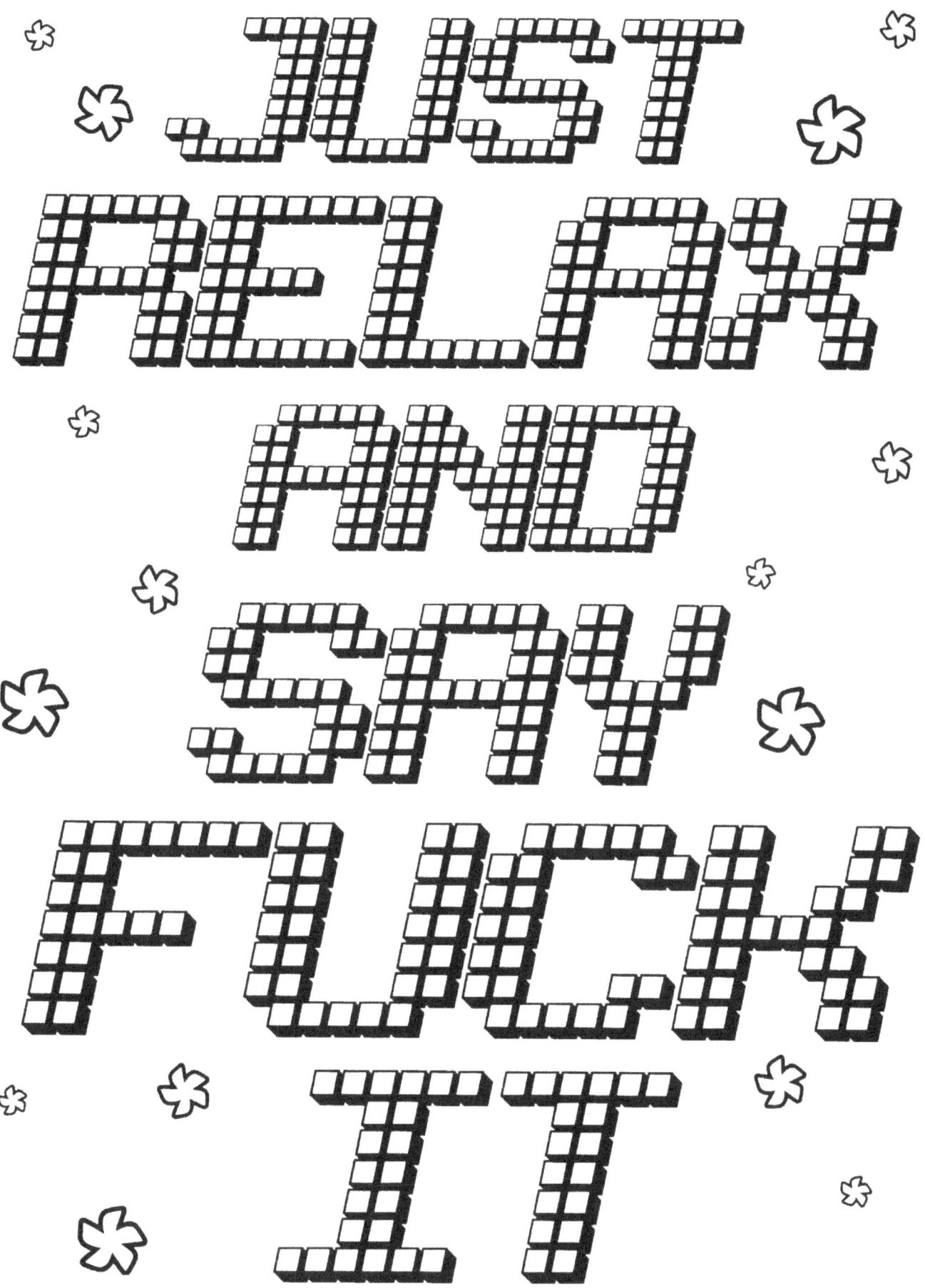

UNFUCK YOURSELF

Be who you were before all that stuff that happened that dimmed your FUCKING SHINE!

I don't have the energy to shit butterflies and piss rainbows today.

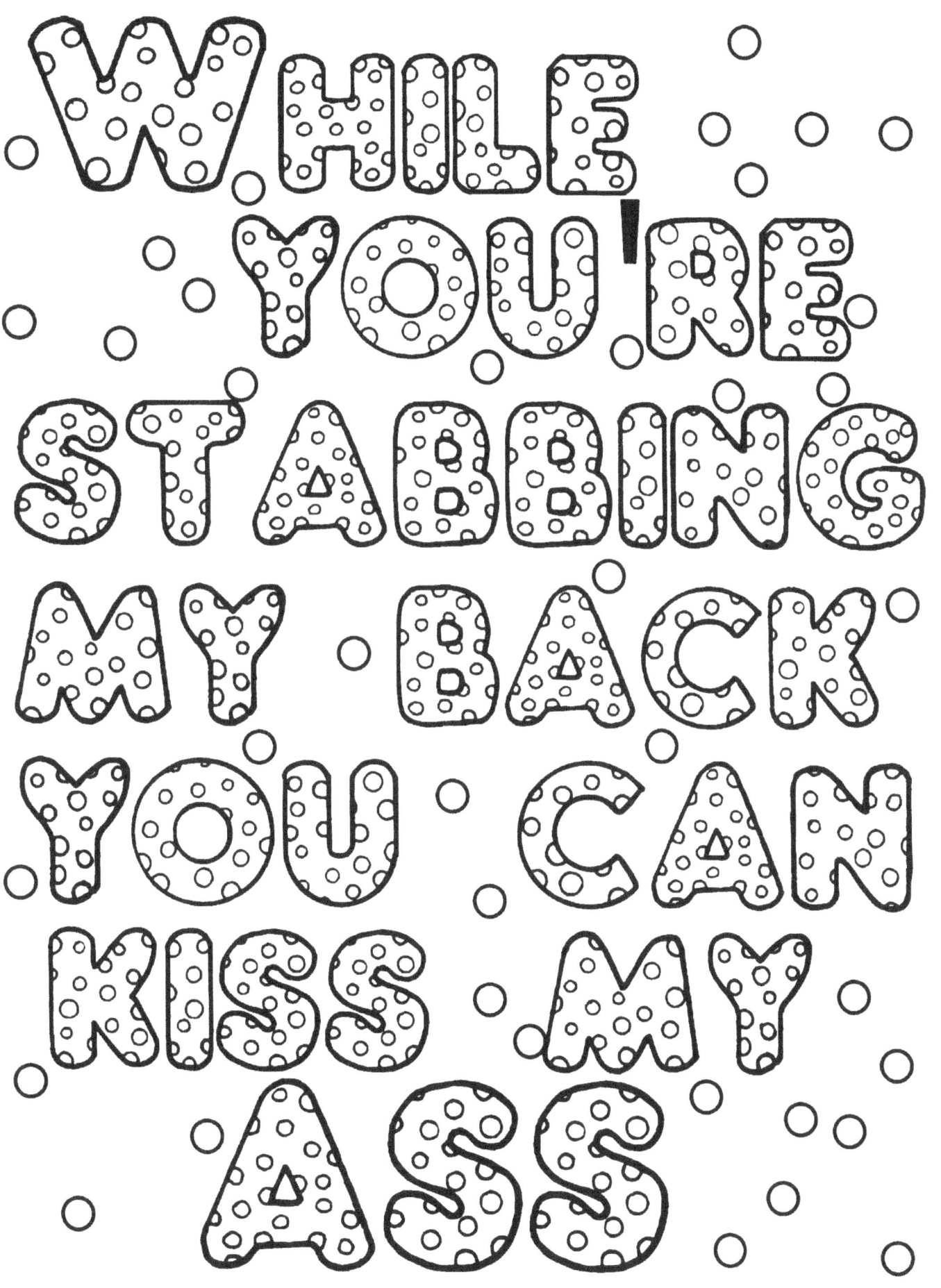

Remember no one is perfect. Everyone's ass has a crack in it.

I SIMPLY USE THE WORD FUCK TO ACCENTUATE MY POINT

I SEE YOUR SILENT TREATMENT AND RAISE YOU A FUCK OFF

BUCKLE UP, BUTTERCUP YOU JUST FLIPPED MY BITCH SWITCH

A good place to put your opinions is up your ASS

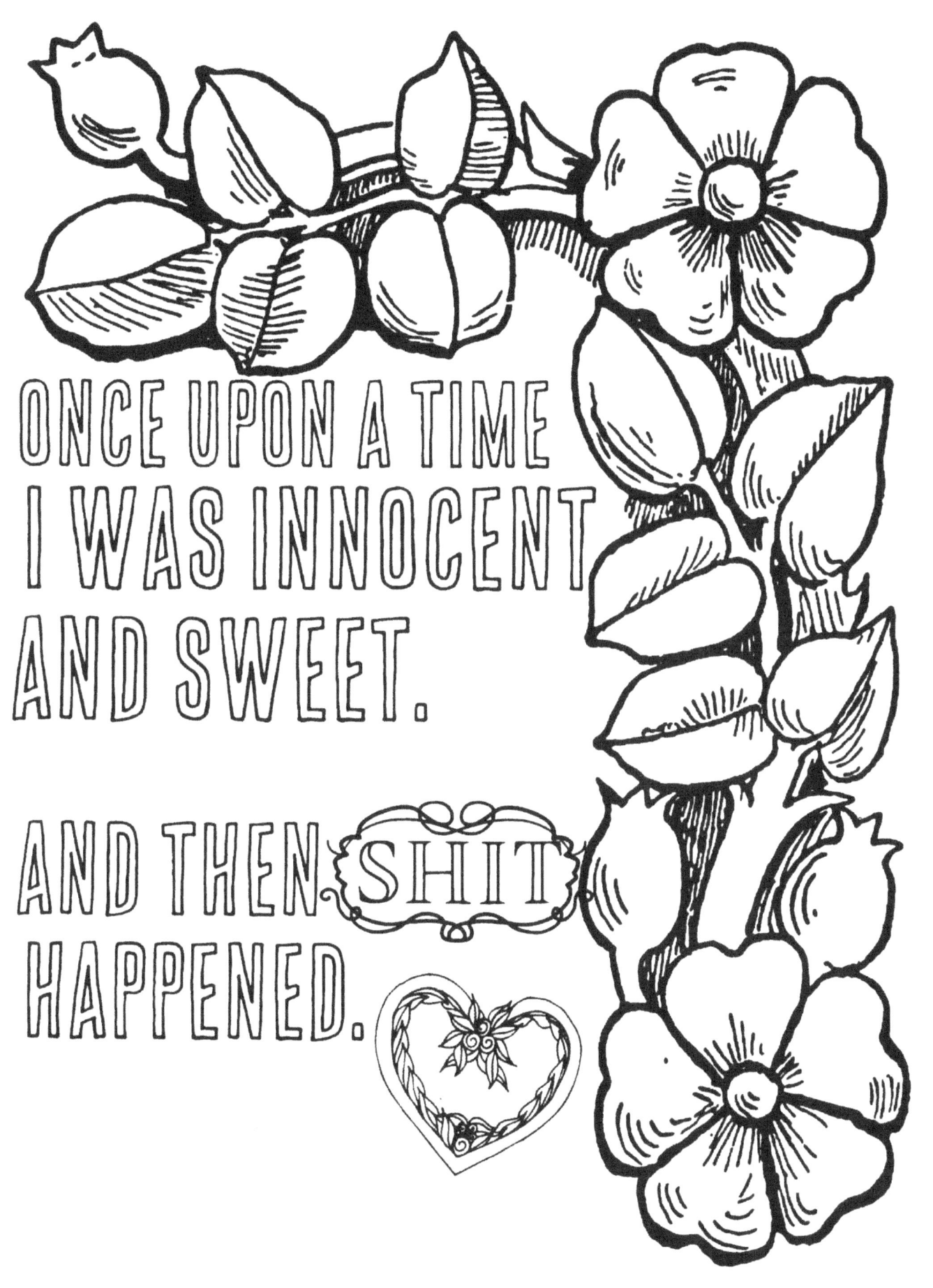

ONCE UPON A TIME
I WAS INNOCENT
AND SWEET.

AND THEN SHIT
HAPPENED.

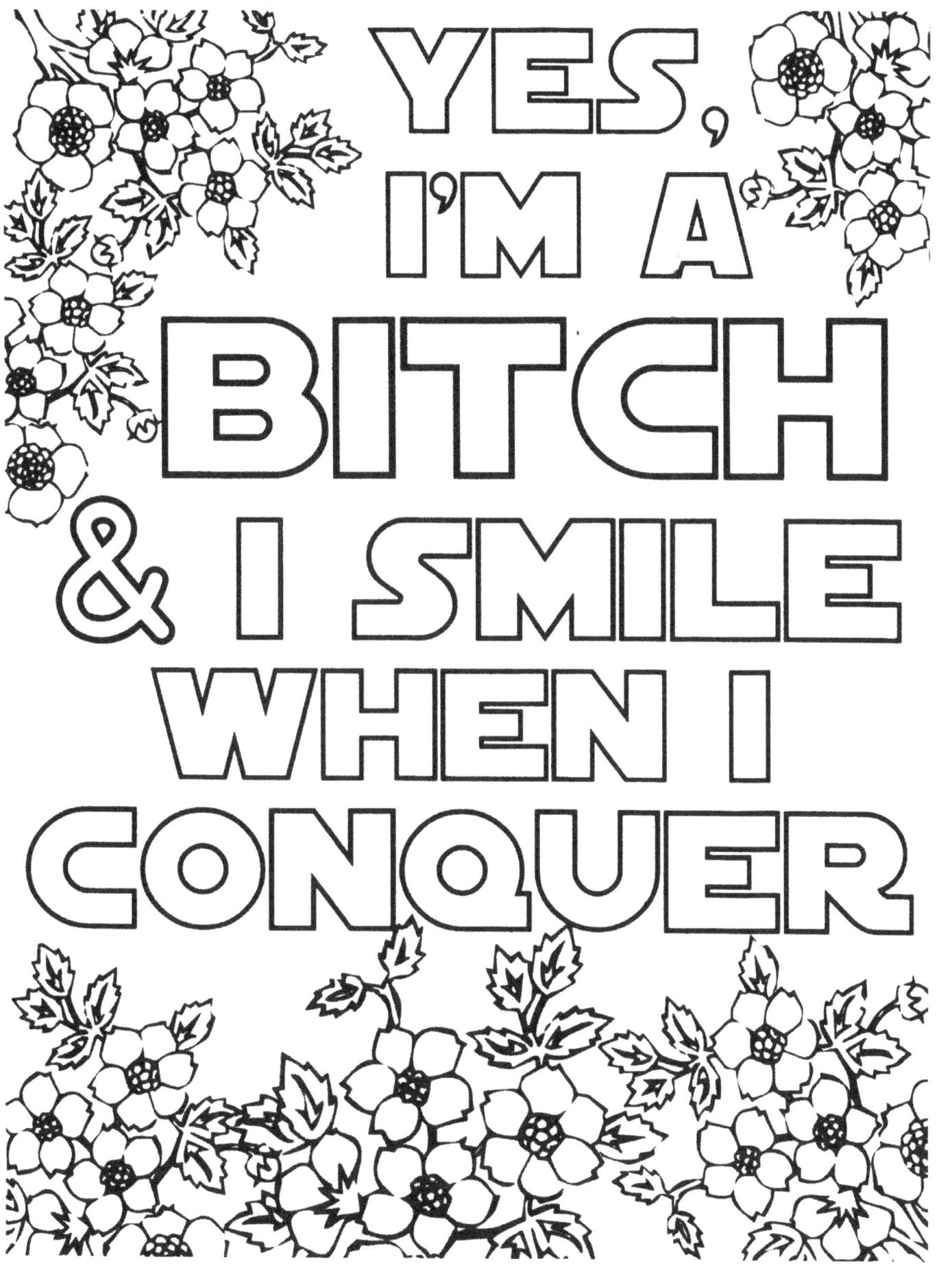

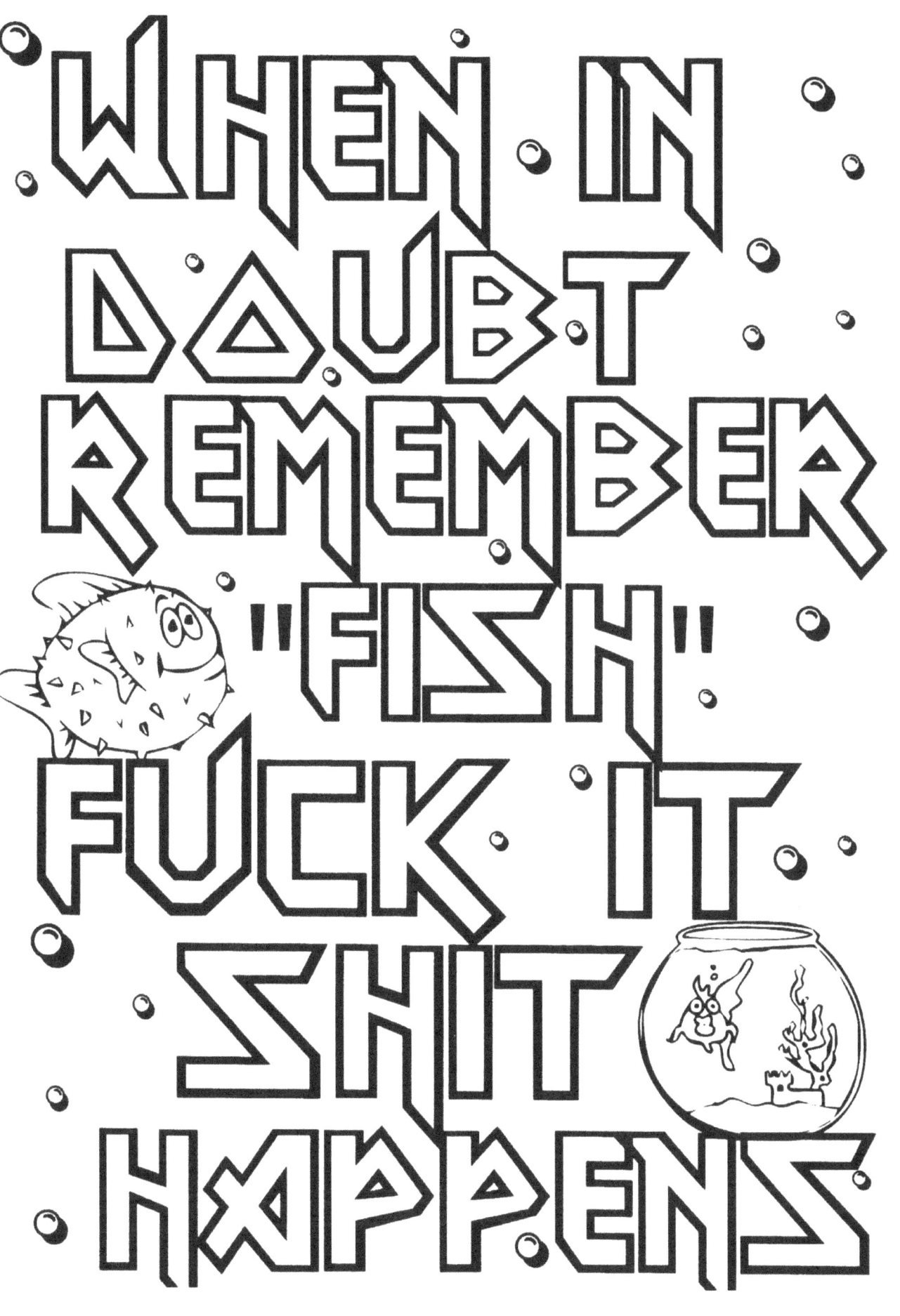

SOMETIMES YOU HAVE TO SAY FUCK IT AND JUST LIVE LIFE

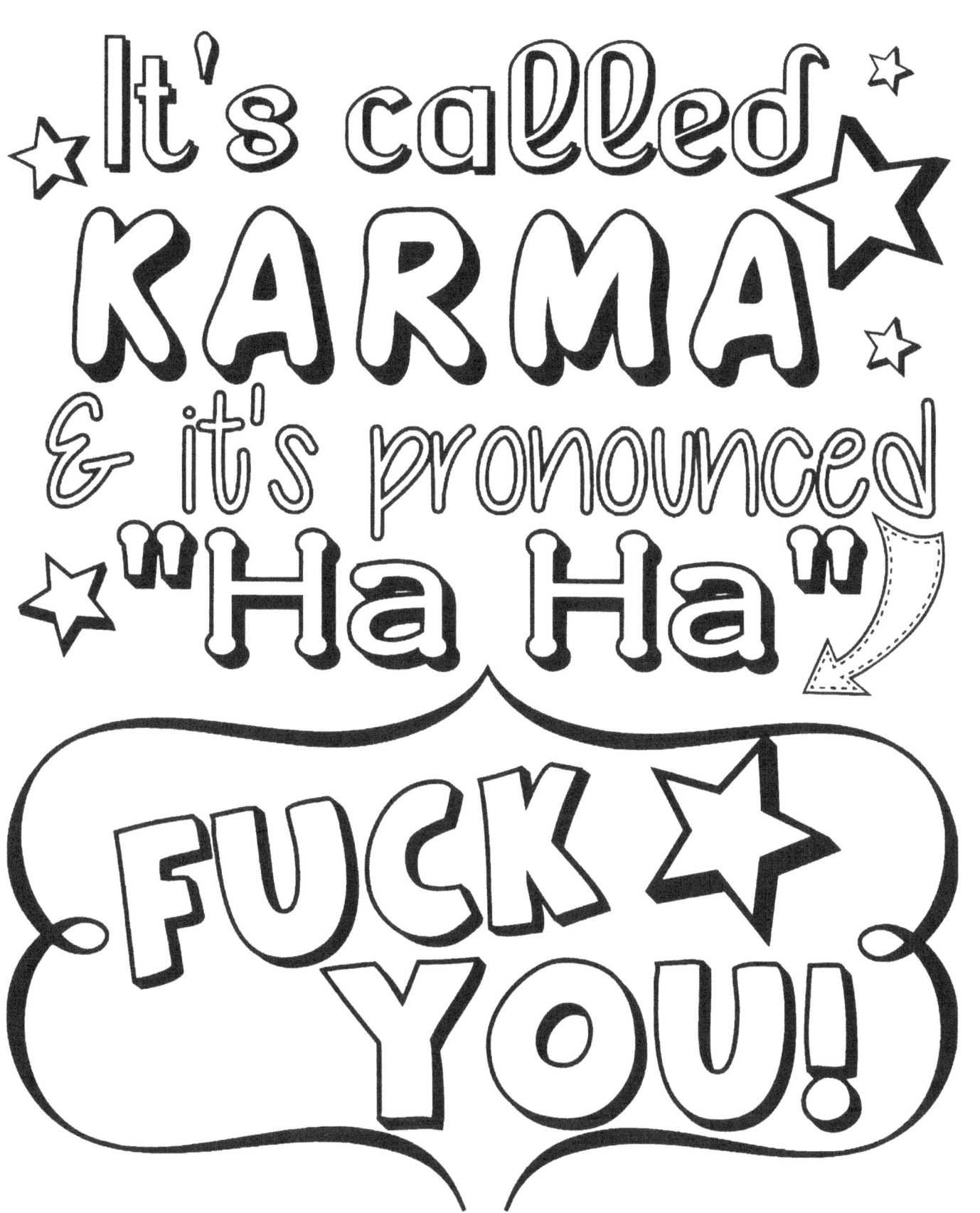

I DON'T SUGAR COAT SHIT, I'M NOT WILLY WONKA.

ONCE
UPON
A TIME
FUCK
YOU
THE END

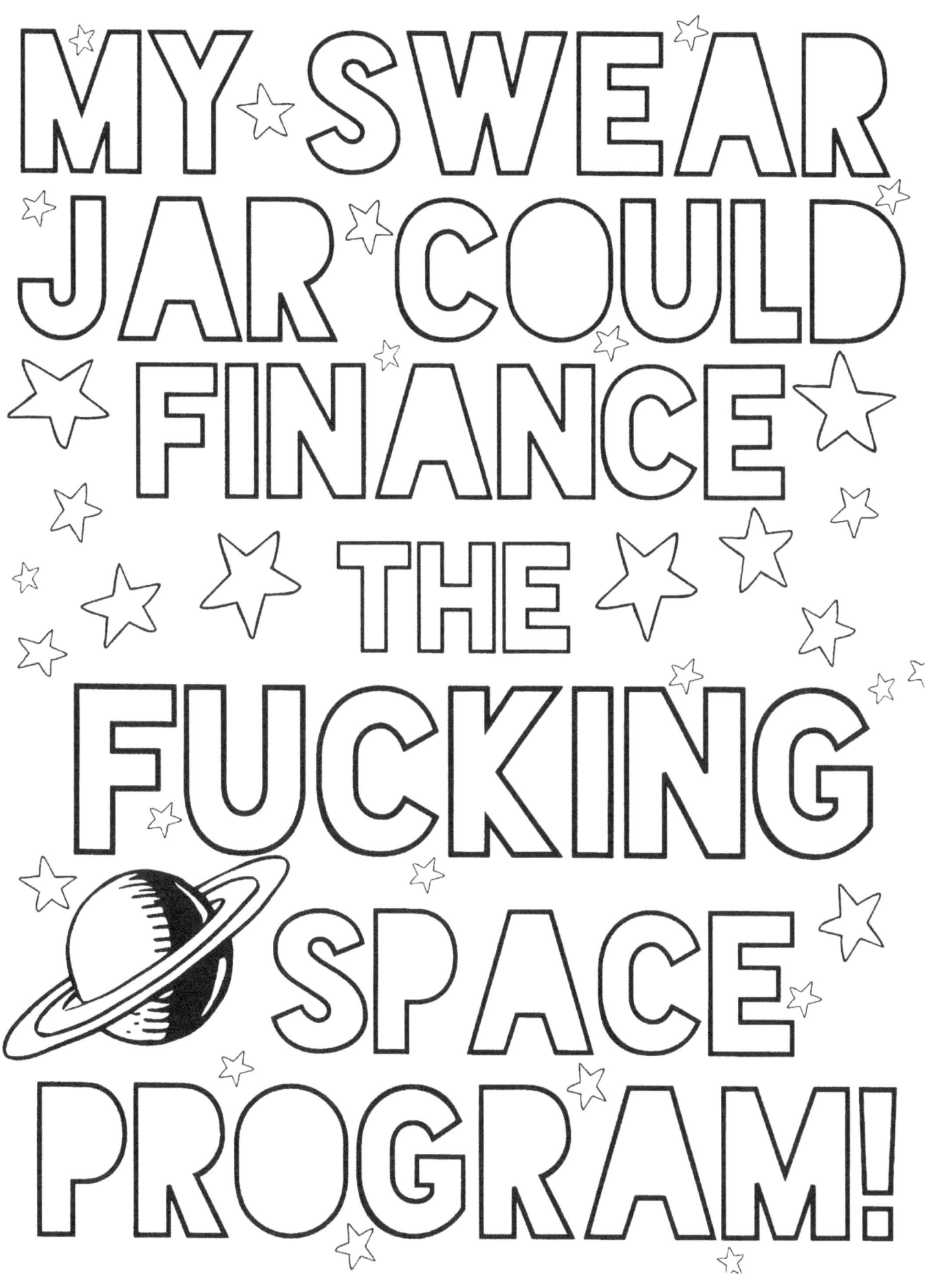

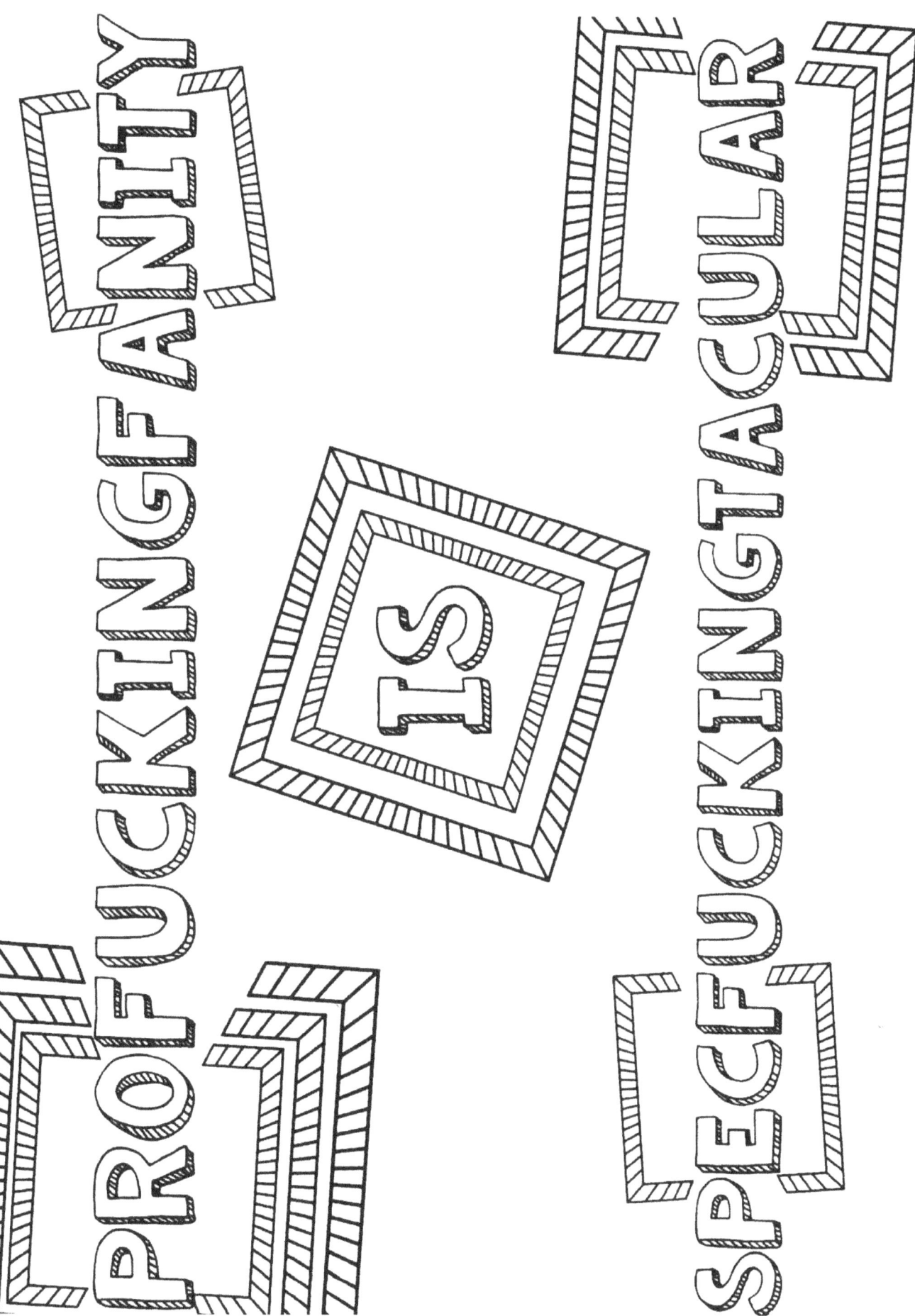

Keep rolling your eyes BITCH, maybe you'll find a brain back there.

ON YOUR MARK, GET SET, GO FUCK YOURSELF

i'm not always a Bitch, just kidding go fuck yourself

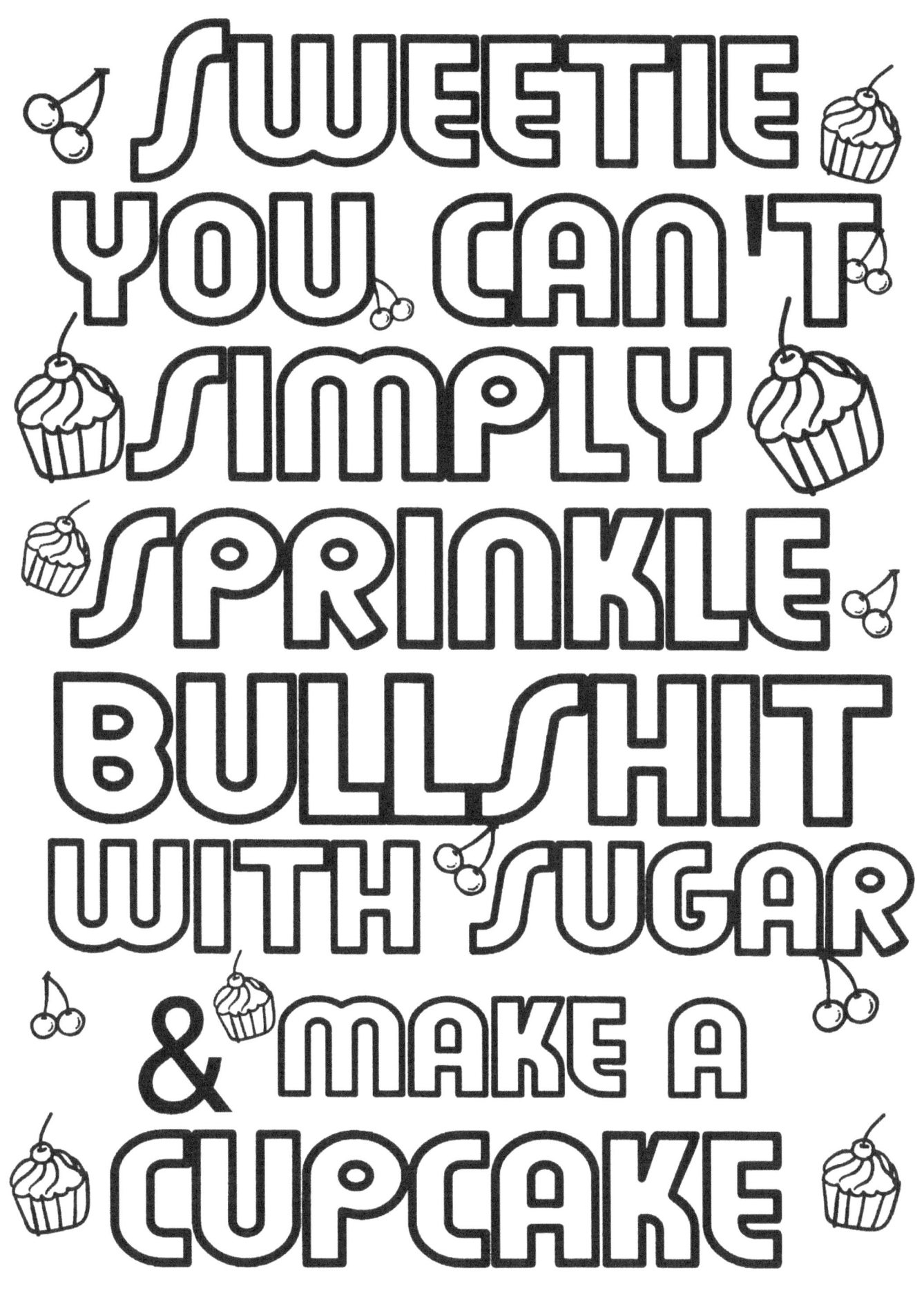

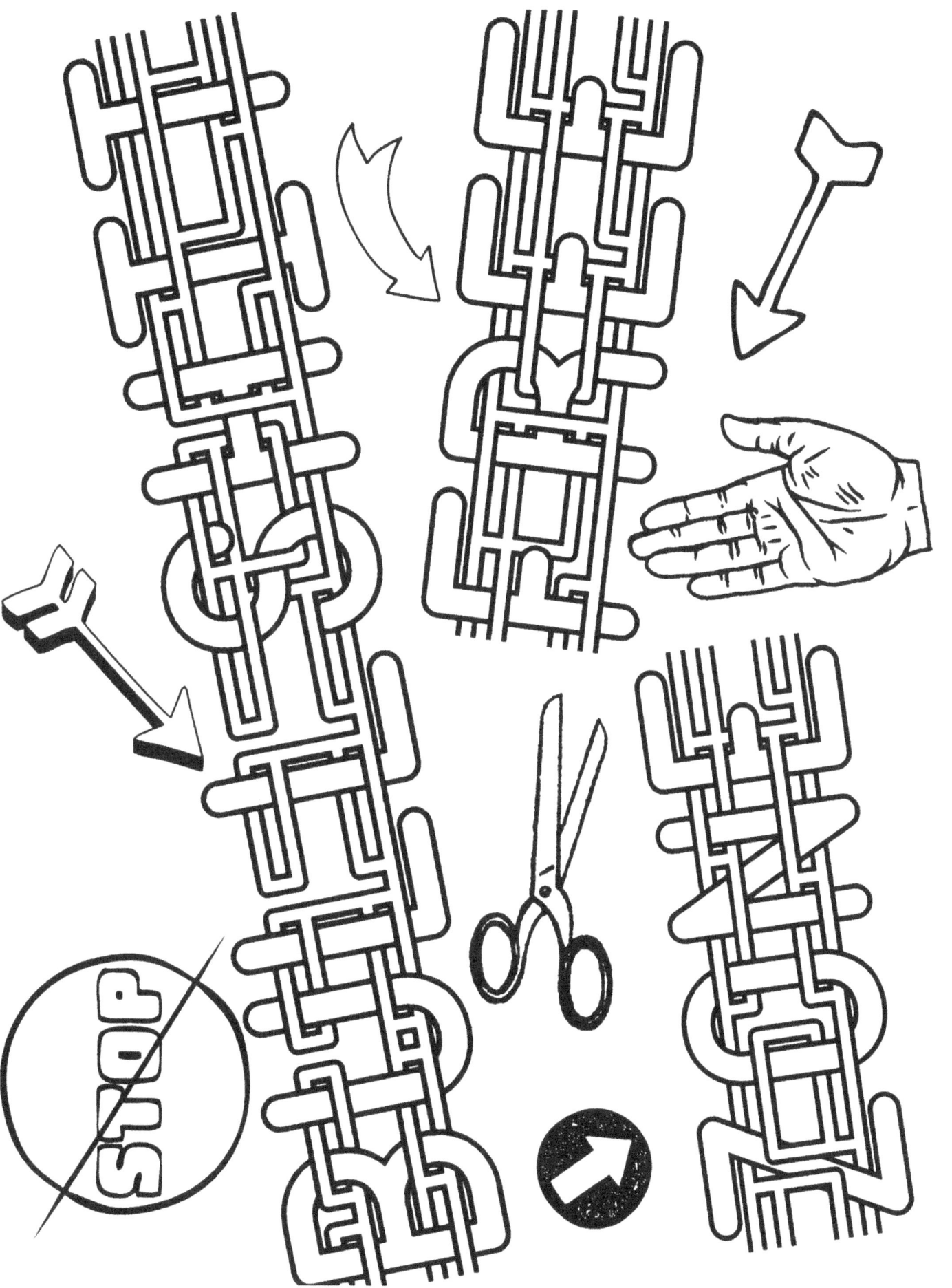

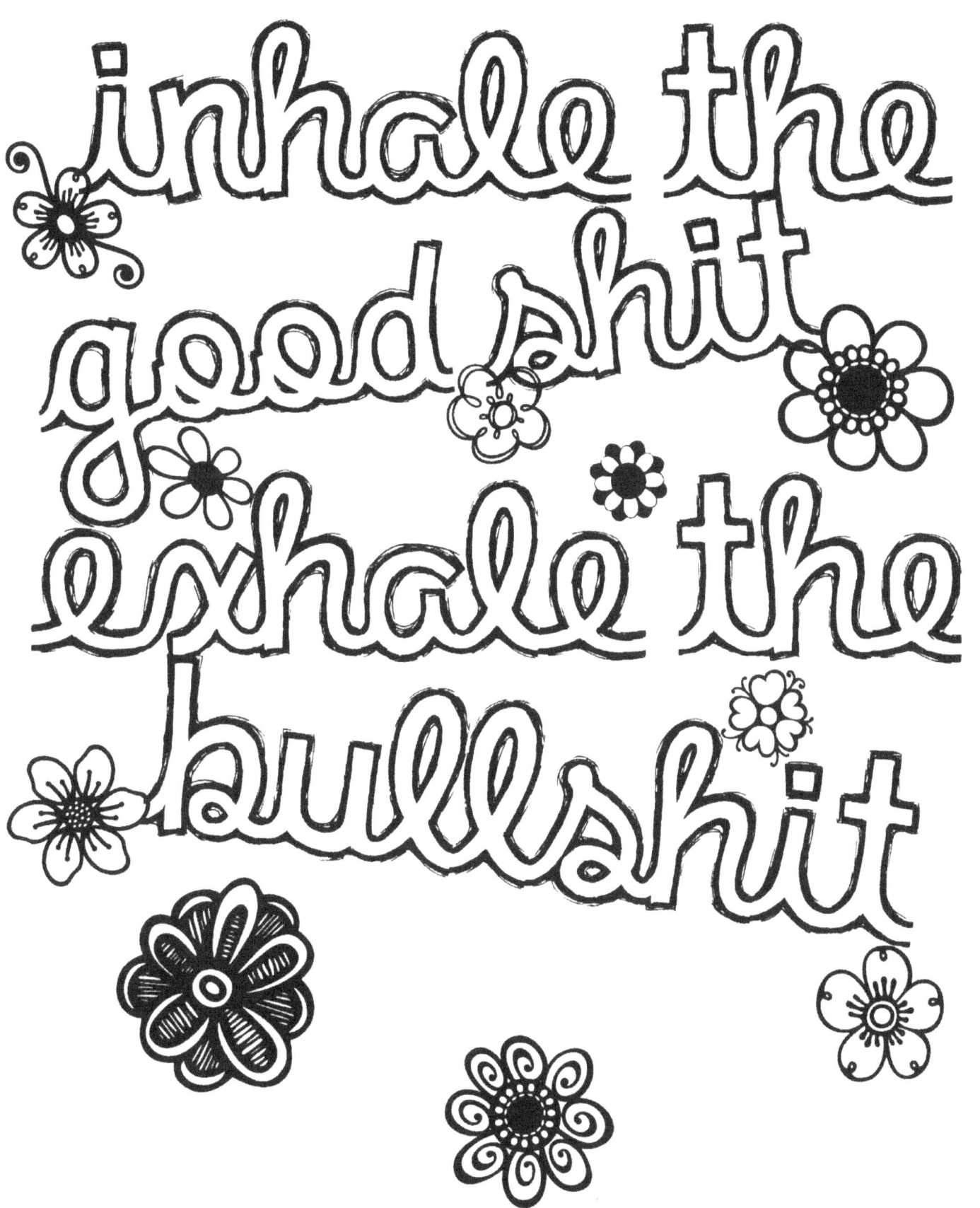

Sometimes even the devil on my shoulder asks "what the FUCK are you doing"

I'M SORRY. WHAT LANGUAGE ARE YOU SPEAKING? IT SOUNDS LIKE BULLSHIT.

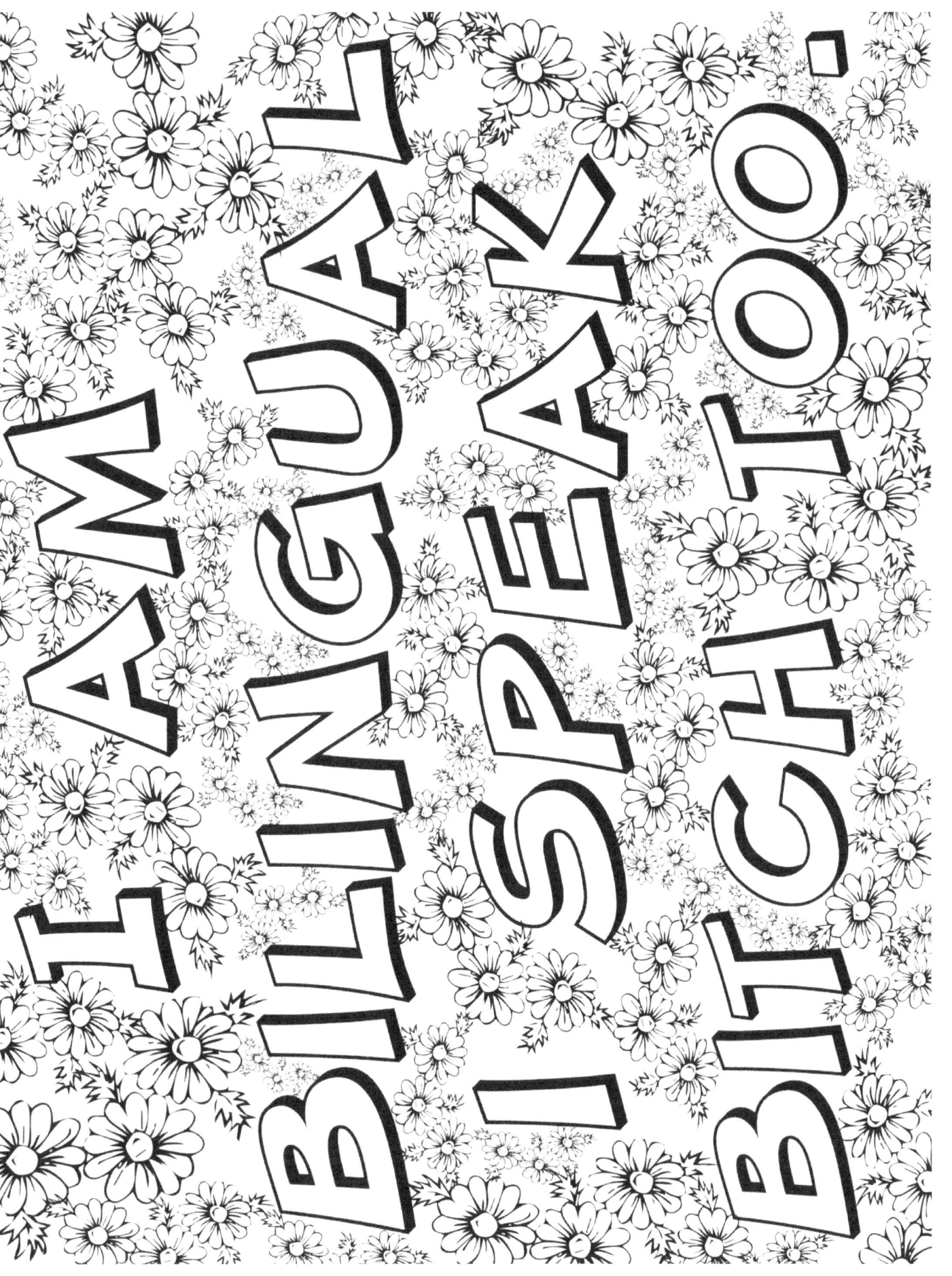

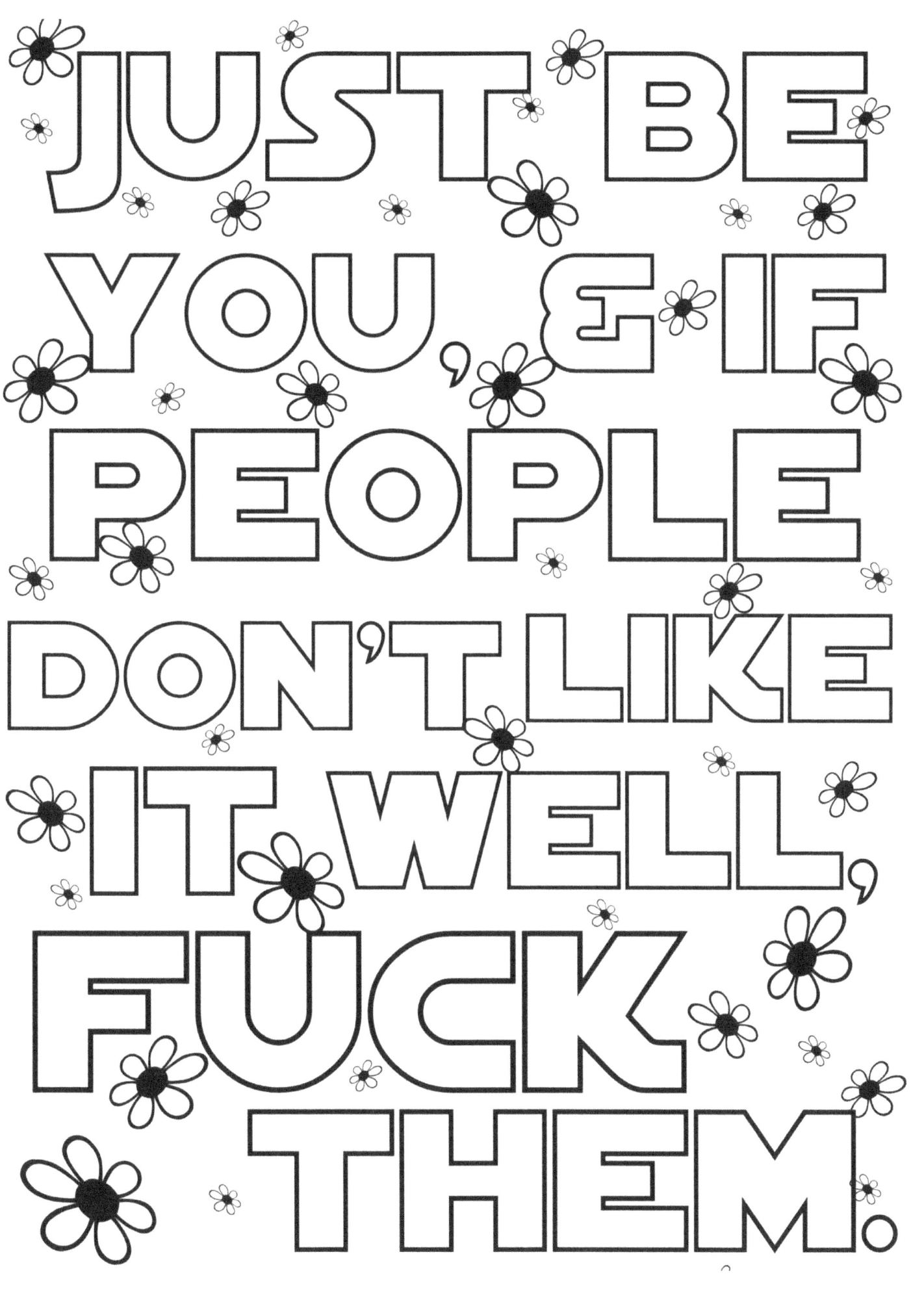

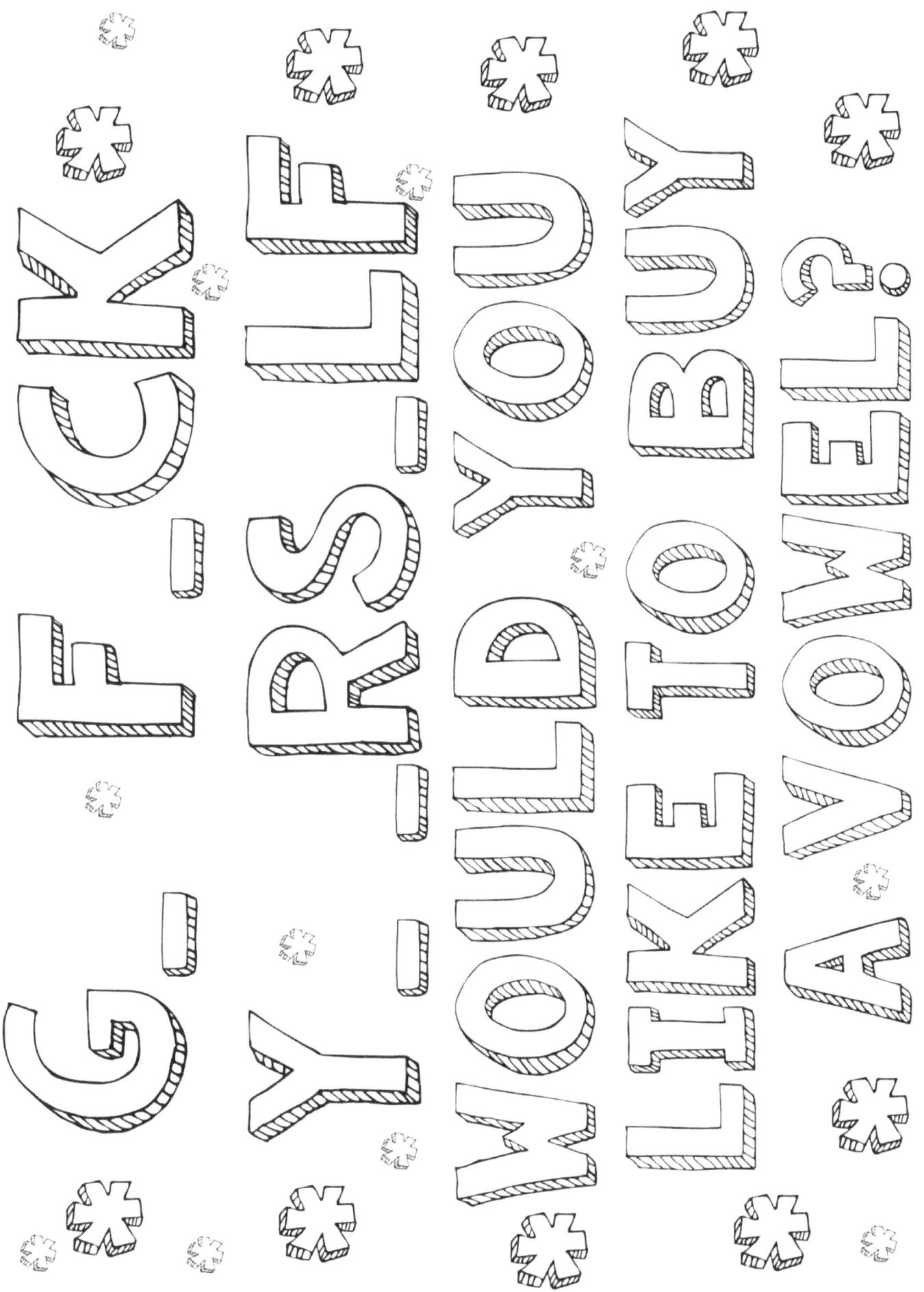

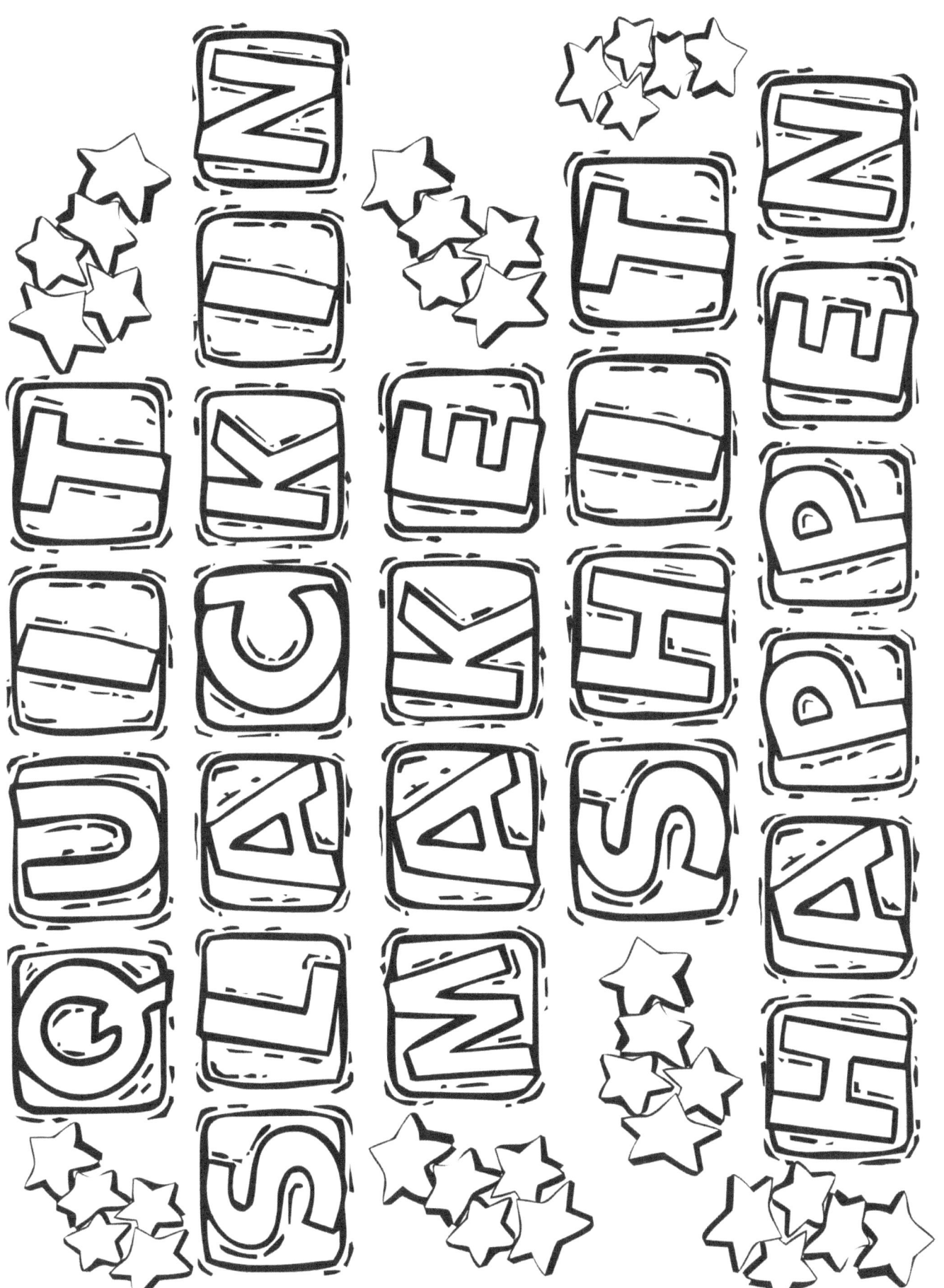

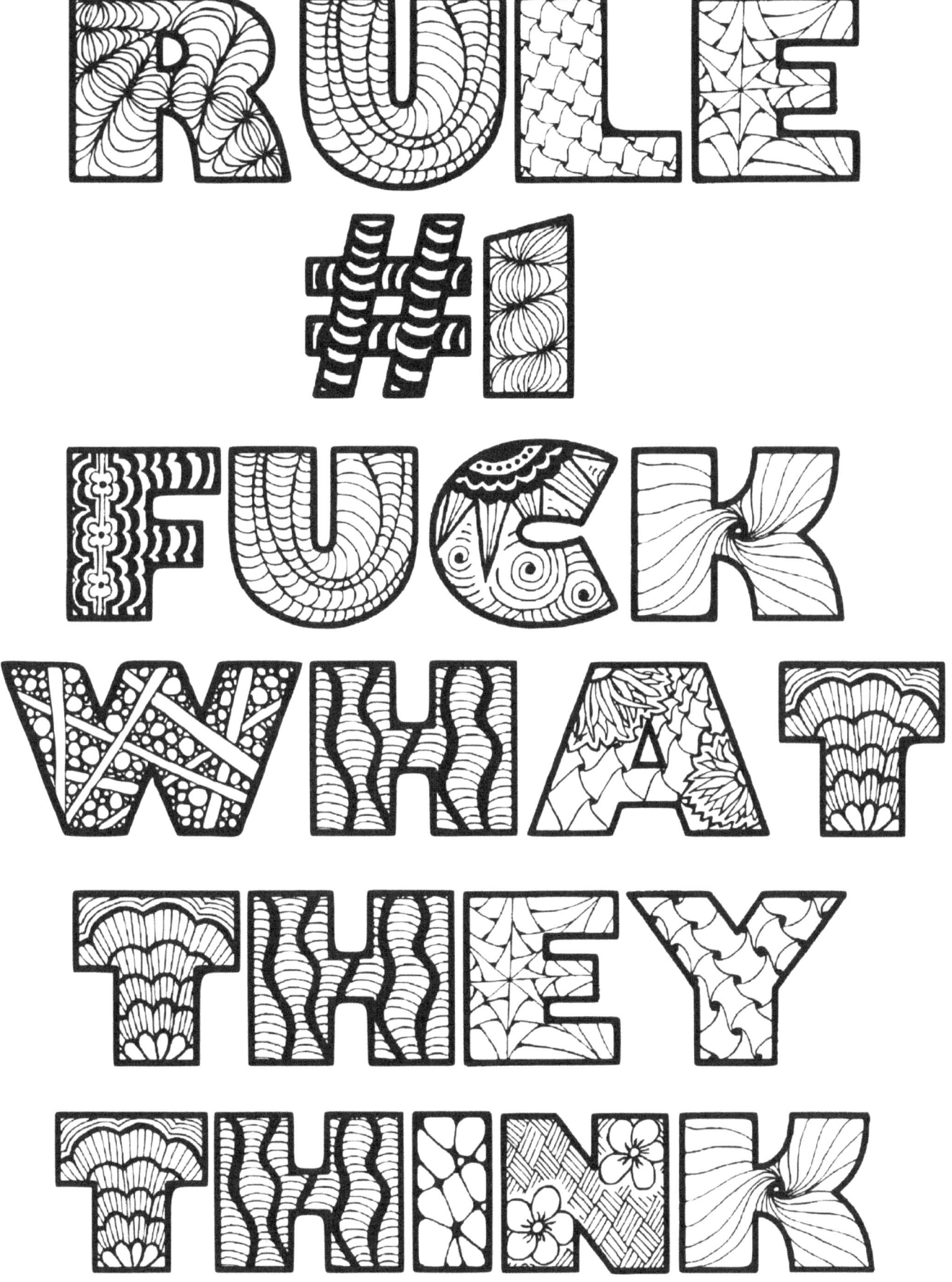

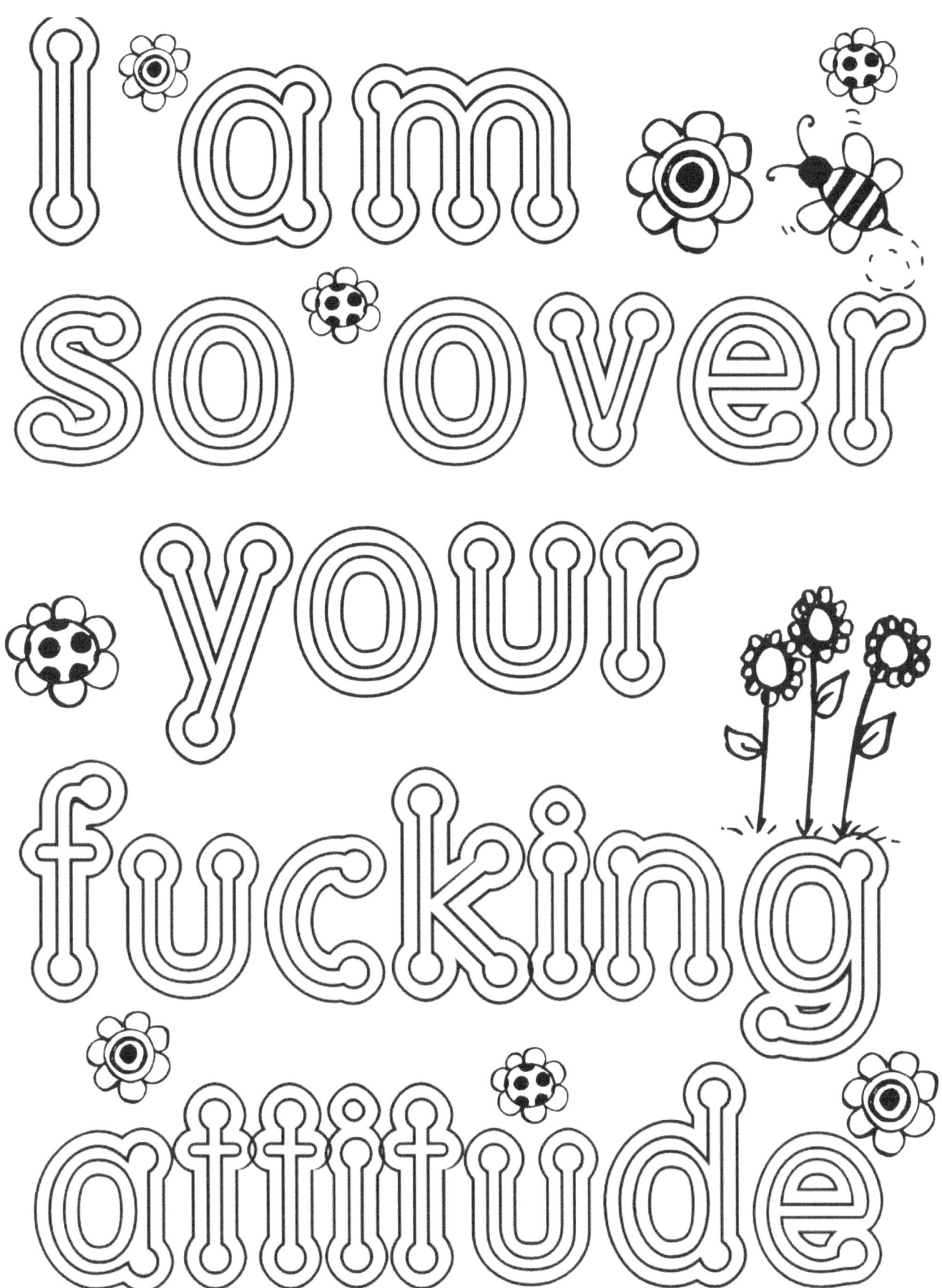

i've come to a point in my life that i need a stronger word than fuck

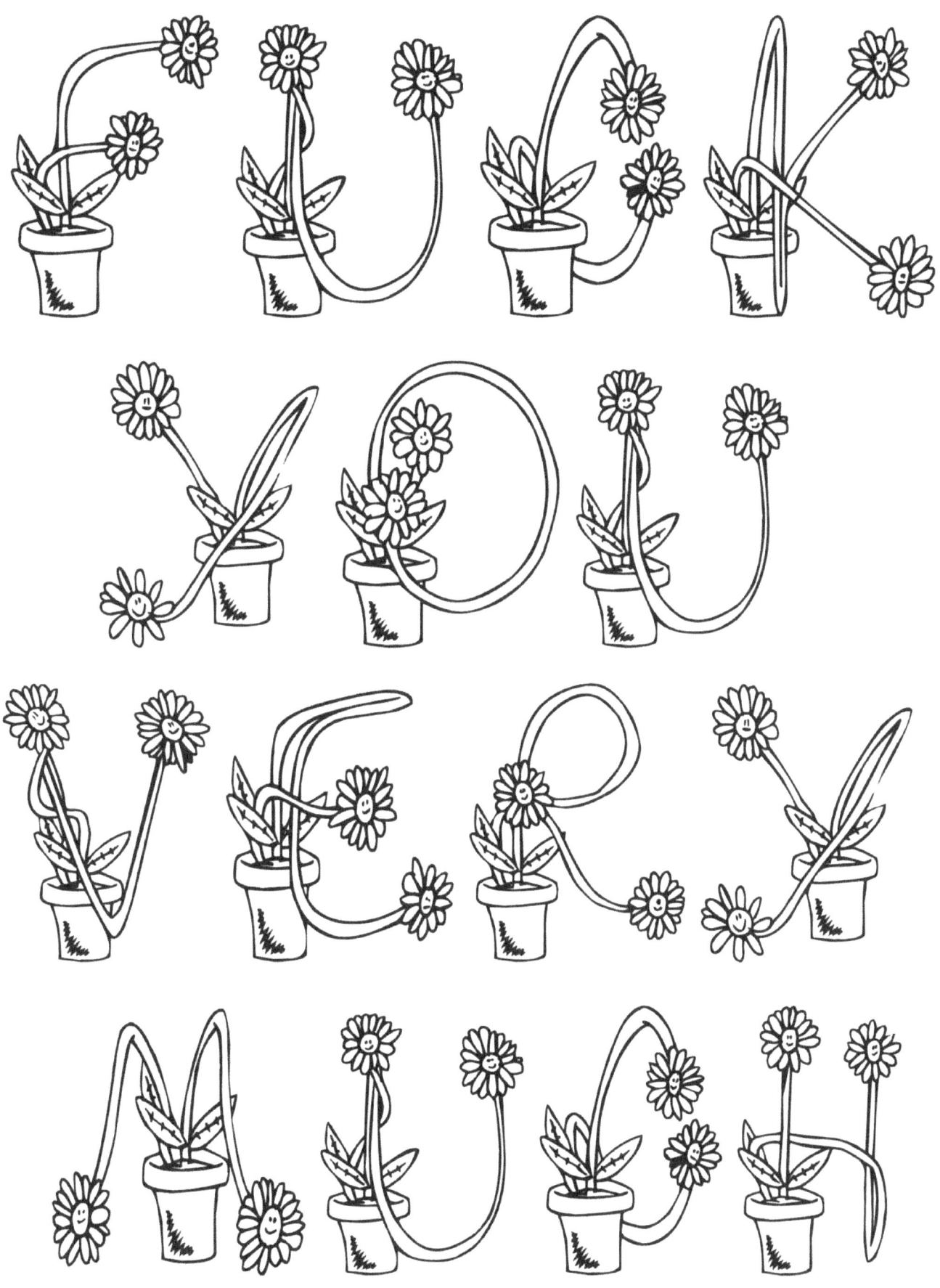

WELL, AREN'T WE JUST A RAY OF FUCKING SUNSHINE

www.ingramcontent.com/pod-product-compliance
Lightning Source LLC
Chambersburg PA
CBHW080627190526
45169CB00009B/3301